HAL•LEONARD
INSTRUMENTAL
PLAY-ALONG

AUDIO
ACCESS
INCLUDED

PLAYBACK+
Speed • Pitch • Balance • Loop

FLUTE

12 POP HITS

T0084970

Audio Arrangements by Peter Deneff

To access audio visit:
www.halleonard.com/mylibrary

8790-2995-1321-5517

ISBN 978-1-5400-2046-8

HAL•LEONARD®
7777 W. BLUEMOUND RD. P.O. BOX 13819 MILWAUKEE, WI 53213

Visit Hal Leonard Online at
www.halleonard.com

BELIEVER

Flute

Words and Music by DAN REYNOLDS,
WAYNE SERMON, BEN McKEE, DANIEL PLATZMAN,
JUSTIN TRANTOR, MATTIAS LARSSON and ROBIN FREDRICKSSON

CAN'T STOP THE FEELING

from TROLLS

Flute

Words and Music by JUSTIN TIMBERLAKE,
MAX MARTIN and SHELLBACK

DESPACITO

Flute

Words and Music by LUIS FONSI,
ERIKA ENDER, JUSTIN BIEBER, JASON BOYD,
MARTY JAMES GARTON and RAMON AYALA

Moderately, in 2

Keyboard

IT AIN'T ME

Flute

Words and Music by ALI TAMPOSI,
SELENA GOMEZ, ANDREW WOTMAN,
KYRRE GORVELL-DAHLL and BRIAN LEE

8

LOOK WHAT YOU MADE ME DO

Flute

8Words and Music by TAYLOR SWIFT,
JACK ANTONOFF, RICHARD FAIRBRASS,
FRED FAIRBRASS and ROB MANZOLI

MILLION REASONS

Flute

Words and Music by STEFANI GERMANOTTA,
MARK RONSON and HILLARY LINDSEY

PERFECT

FLUTE

Words and Music by
ED SHEERAN

SEND MY LOVE
(To Your New Lover)

Flute

Words and Music by ADELE ADKINS,
MAX MARTIN and SHELLBACK

SHAPE OF YOU

Flute

Words and Music by ED SHEERAN,
KEVIN BRIGGS, KANDI BURRUSS, TAMEKA COTTLE,
STEVE MAC and JOHNNY McDAID

SLOW HANDS

flute

Words and Music by NIALL HORAN,
JOHN HENRY RYAN, ALEXANDER IZQUIERDO,
RUTH-ANNE CUNNINGHAM, TOBIAS JESSO JR.
and JULIAN BUNETTA

TOO GOOD AT GOODBYES

Flute

Words and Music by SAM SMITH,
TOR HERMANSEN, MIKKEL ERIKSEN
and JAMES NAPIER

WHAT ABOUT US

FLUTE

Words and Music by ALECIA MOORE, STEVE MAC and JOHNNY McDAID